# EVERYDAY
# British

## The heart-healthy way to make over 60 of your favourite recipes

SIMON &
SCHUSTER
ILLUSTRATED

First published in Great Britain in 2012 by Simon & Schuster UK Ltd
A CBS COMPANY

1   3   5   7   9   10   8   6   4   2

SIMON & SCHUSTER
ILLUSTRATED BOOKS
Simon & Schuster UK Ltd
222 Gray's Inn Road
London
WC1X 8HB

www.simonandschuster.co.uk

Simon & Schuster Australia, Sydney
Simon & Schuster India, New Delhi

Editorial director: Francine Lawrence
Senior commissioning editor: Nicky Hill
Project editor: Salima Hirani
Designer: Geoff Fennell
BHF Senior dietitian: Victoria Taylor
Photography: William Shaw
Styling and photography art direction: Tony Hutchinson
Food styling: Sara Lewis
Production manager: Katherine Thornton
Commercial director: Ami Richards

A CIP catalogue record for this book is available from the British Library

ISBN 978-1-47110-230-1

Printed and bound in Italy
Colour reproduction by Dot Gradations Ltd, UK

# Contents

# Muffins with leeks & cheese

**Serves: 2**
**Preparation time: 10 minutes**
**Cooking time: 15 minutes**

**1½ teaspoons olive oil**

**2 leeks, trimmed, washed and thinly sliced**

**2 English muffins (white or wholemeal)**

**40g (1½oz) half-fat mature Cheddar-style cheese, finely grated**

**1 decent-sized spring onion, finely chopped**

**½ teaspoon Dijon mustard, or to taste**

**1 tablespoon finely chopped fresh parsley**

**Freshly ground black pepper, to taste**

**A delicious dish that makes a satisfying breakfast or brunch. Or try these tasty savoury muffins as a healthy alternative to sweet treats on baking days.**

1 Heat the olive oil in a frying pan, then add the leeks and cook over a medium-high heat for 7–10 minutes or until softened and slightly browned, stirring frequently. Spoon the cooked leek into a bowl and set aside.

2 Preheat the grill to medium-high. Split the muffins in half and place them on a baking tray. Lightly toast them under the grill, cut-sides down. Turn the muffin halves over. Add the cheese, spring onion, mustard, parsley and black pepper to the leeks and mix well. Spoon some of the leek mixture over each muffin half, dividing it evenly between all 4. Return the topped muffins to the grill for a few minutes until lightly browned, then serve immediately, with grilled tomato halves or roasted cherry tomatoes.

**Variation:** Fresh bagels or crumpets (2 crumpets per serving, and don't cut them in half) can be substituted for the muffins.

| per 100g | MED **fat** | MED **saturated fat** | MED **salt** | LOW **sugar** |
|---|---|---|---|---|
| per portion (% of GDA) | **300 kcal** 15% | **9.5g fat** 14% | **3g saturated fat** 15% | **1.4g salt** 23% | **5g sugars** 6% |

# Porridge with mixed berry compote

**Serves: 4**
**Preparation time: 5 minutes**
**Cooking time: 10 minutes**

115g (4oz) porridge oats
400ml (14fl oz) semi-skimmed milk
400ml (14fl oz) water

**For the compote:**

3 tablespoons unsweetened red
   grape juice

3 tablespoons unsweetened
   apple juice

1 tablespoon clear runny honey

350g (12oz) mixed fresh berries,
   such as raspberries, blackberries,
   blueberries and small strawberries
   (halved)

The whole family will love this fruity breakfast. Make extra compote for the freezer so you always have some handy for a lightening-quick breakfast.

1  To make the fruit compote, place the fruit juices and honey in a saucepan and heat until almost boiling, stirring. Remove the pan from the heat. Place the mixed berries in a bowl and pour the hot fruit juice mixture over them. Stir gently to mix the ingredients, then set aside. Serve the compote warm, at room temperature or chilled, according to your preference.

2  To make the porridge, place the oats in a non-stick saucepan and stir in the milk and water. Bring gently to the boil, stirring all the time, then simmer for 3–5 minutes or until the desired consistency is achieved, stirring occasionally. Serve the porridge immediately, with the compote spooned on top.

| per 100g | LOW fat | LOW saturated fat | LOW salt | LOW sugar |
|---|---|---|---|---|
| per portion (% of GDA) | **214 kcal** 11% | **4.5g fat** 6% | **1.2g saturated fat** 6% | **0.3g salt** 5% | **16.1g sugars** 18% |

# Winter fruit compote

This seasonal alternative to the compote on the opposite page has a cosy Christmassy flavour. Serve it by itself, or on some porridge or yoghurt.

1  Put the dried fruit in a bowl. Pour the juices into a jug, add the mixed spice and whisk together. Now add the juice to the fruit and mix well. Cover and chill in the refrigerator for several hours or overnight.

2  If serving the compote cold, remove it from the refrigerator and allow it to stand at room temperature for about 1 hour before serving. If serving warm, transfer the fruit and juices to a small pan and heat gently, stirring occasionally. (Alternatively, put the compote in a microwave-safe container, cover loosely and heat in a microwave oven on a high setting for about 2 minutes or until hot, stirring once.) Remove from heat and allow to cool slightly before serving.

3  Divide the compote between 2 serving bowls, sprinkle with the flaked almonds (if using) and serve on its own or topped with a little low-fat natural yoghurt.

**Variations:** Ground cinnamon can be substituted for the mixed spice. Try sprinkling the compote with toasted seeds instead of the flaked almonds.

**Cook's tip:** Try snipping the dried fruit into pieces with scissors before adding the juice.

Serves: **2–3**
Preparation time: **10 minutes, plus overnight chilling**
Cooking time: **5 minutes, if serving warm**

**225g (8oz) mixed dried fruit of your choice or dried fruit salad, such as apricots, pitted prunes, peaches, pears and apple rings**

**100ml (3½fl oz) unsweetened apple juice**

**100ml (3½fl oz) unsweetened orange juice**

**½ teaspoon mixed spice**

**10g (¼oz) toasted flaked almonds (optional)**

| per 100g | LOW fat | LOW saturated fat | LOW salt | MED sugar |
|---|---|---|---|---|
| per portion (% of GDA) | **138 kcal** 7% | **0.5g fat** 1% | **0g saturated fat** 0% | **0g salt** 0% | **33g sugars** 37% |

# Lemon-blueberry pancakes

**Serves: 2 (makes 8 mini pancakes)**
**Preparation time: 15 minutes**
**Cooking time: 10–15 minutes**

**55g (2oz) self-raising flour**
**15g (½oz) caster sugar**
**1 teaspoon finely grated lemon zest**
**4 tablespoons semi-skimmed milk**
**1 egg**
**55g (2oz) fresh blueberries**
**1½ teaspoons sunflower oil**

**For the lemon-blueberry sauce:**
**40g (1½oz) caster sugar**
**4 tablespoons water**
**55g (2oz) fresh blueberries**
**1 tablespoon freshly squeezed
     lemon juice**

*Pancakes are a delicious option when you're in the mood for
a breakfast treat. Vary the berries each time for colourful twist.*

1   First make the sauce. Put the sugar and water in a small saucepan and heat
    gently, stirring, until the sugar has dissolved. Add the blueberries, bring to
    the boil and bubble over a medium heat for 2–4 minutes until the syrup
    has thickened slightly. Stir in the lemon juice and heat again until bubbling.
    Remove from the heat and keep warm.

2   Make the pancakes. Sift the flour into a bowl, then stir in the sugar and
    lemon zest. Add the milk and egg and whisk to make a smooth batter.
    Stir in the blueberries.

3   Heat the oil in a large non-stick frying pan. Spoon 4 dollops of the batter
    (to make 4 mini pancakes) onto the frying pan – ensure you keep them
    apart. Cook over a medium heat for 2–3 minutes, then carefully turn over
    the pancakes and cook for 1–2 minutes until golden brown. Transfer to
    a warmed plate and keep warm while you cook the next 4 pancakes.

4   Place 4 pancakes on each serving plate, drizzle over the sauce and
    serve immediately.

    **Cook's tip:** If you prefer larger pancakes, make 4 in total and serve
    2 pancakes per portion.

| per 100g | MED fat | LOW saturated fat | LOW salt | MED sugar |
|---|---|---|---|---|
| per portion (% of GDA) | **343 kcal** 17% | **12g fat** 17% | **2g saturated fat** 10% | **0.2g salt** 3% | **34g sugars** 38% |

# Cinnamon fruit toast

**Serves: 2**
**Preparation time: 10 minutes**
**Cooking time: 5 minutes**

1½–2 teaspoons caster sugar

¼ teaspoon ground cinnamon,
   or to taste

1 banana

2 medium or 4 small slices fruit bread

2 teaspoons low-fat or reduced-fat
   sunflower spread

55g (2oz) fresh raspberries or
   blueberries

10g (¼oz) toasted flaked almonds
   (optional)

**This delicious dish is good on any day, but is special enough for the perfect healthy celebration breakfast.**

1 Combine the sugar and cinnamon in a small bowl and set aside. Peel the banana, cut it diagonally into 10–12 even slices and set aside.

2 Toast the fruit bread on both sides in a toaster or under a preheated grill. Spread the hot toast slices with sunflower spread, then sprinkle most of the cinnamon sugar evenly over the toast, reserving a little of the cinnamon sugar for serving.

3 Arrange the banana slices on the toast, then sprinkle with the reserved cinnamon sugar. Sprinkle with the fresh berries and flaked almonds (if using). Serve immediately.

**Variations:** 1–2 fresh ripe pears (cored and sliced) can be substituted for the banana. Try using mixed-seed bread or halved teacakes instead of the fruit bread.

| per 100g | MED fat | LOW saturated fat | LOW salt | MED sugar |
|---|---|---|---|---|
| per portion (% of GDA) | 233 kcal 12% | 5.4g fat 8% | 0.3g saturated fat 2% | 0.4g salt 7% | 28g sugars 31% |

# Apricot muesli with toasted seeds

**Serves: 10 x 100g (3½oz) portions**
**Preparation time: 5–10 minutes**
**Cooking time: 5 minutes**

**40g (1½oz) sunflower seeds**
**280g (10oz) ready-to-eat dried
  apricots**
**165g (5¾oz) jumbo rolled oats**
**140g (5oz) wheat flakes**
**100g (3½oz) barley flakes**
**75g (2¾oz) rye flakes**
**200g (7oz) sultanas, chopped**

**Apricots are delicious in this muesli, and the toasted sunflower seeds provide a tasty savoury crunch.**

1 Toast the sunflower seeds in a non-stick pan over a medium-high heat for about 5 minutes, stirring frequently. Remove the seeds from the pan and allow them to cool completely.

2 Use clean kitchen scissors to snip the apricots into pieces.

3 Place the oats, wheat flakes, barley flakes, rye flakes and sunflower seeds in a large bowl and stir to mix. Add the dried fruit and mix well.

4 Transfer the muesli to an airtight container and cover tightly. Serve with milk or low-fat natural yoghurt and top with a little prepared fresh fruit, such as blueberries or raspberries.

**Variations:** Bran flakes, bran sticks or buckwheat flakes can be substituted for the barley or rye flakes. Try using other mixed dried fruit, such as ready-to-eat dried pears and raisins, or ready-to-eat dried figs and cranberries, in place of the apricots and sultanas. Pumpkin seeds can be substituted for the sunflower seeds.

| per 100g | MED fat | LOW saturated fat | MED salt | MED sugar |
|---|---|---|---|---|
| per portion (% of GDA) | **286 kcal** 14% | **4.3g fat** 6% | **0.6g saturated fat** 3% | **0.6g salt** 10% | **29g sugars** 32% |

# Banana yoghurt smoothie

Starting the day with this filling smoothie allows you to tick off one of your five-a-day first thing in the morning.

1 Place the bananas, yoghurt, milk and honey in the bowl of a blender or food processor and blend until smooth and well mixed.

2 Add the cinnamon and blend once more to incorporate it. Pour the smoothie into glasses and serve immediately.

   **Variation:** Ground ginger or nutmeg can be substituted for the cinnamon, if desired.

**Serves: 2 (makes about 600ml/20fl oz)**
**Preparation time: 10 minutes**
**Cooking time: none**

**2 medium bananas, cut into chunks**

**200ml (7fl oz) low-fat natural yoghurt**

**125ml (4fl oz) semi-skimmed milk**

**2 tablespoons clear (runny) honey, or to taste**

**¼ teaspoon ground cinnamon, or to taste**

| per 100g | LOW fat | | LOW saturated fat | | LOW salt | | MED sugar | |
|---|---|---|---|---|---|---|---|---|
| per portion (% of GDA) | **285 kcal** 14% | **2.5g fat** 4% | **1.25g saturated fat** 6% | | **0.3g salt** 5% | | **57g sugars** 63% | |

# Light
# BITES

# Sardine pâté

This highly nutritious and tasty light lunch or starter takes just minutes to prepare and is so easy to put together.

1 Drain the sardines, discarding the oil. Place the sardines in a bowl and mash well (bones and all).

2 Add 2 tablespoons of the fromage frais and the horseradish sauce, lemon zest, parsley (if using) and black pepper and mix well. Add the remaining tablespoon of fromage frais, if desired. Serve the spread on top of crusty French bread, hot toast or crackers, or as a dip with fresh vegetable crudités and breadsticks.

Variation: Use another canned fish, such as mackerel or pilchards, in place of the sardines, and vary the seasonings according to taste.

**Serves: 2**
**Preparation time: 15 minutes**
**Cooking time: none**

**125g (4½oz) can sardines in sunflower oil**

**2–3 tablespoons virtually fat-free natural fromage frais**

**2 teaspoons hot horseradish sauce**

**1 teaspoon finely grated lemon zest**

**2 teaspoons finely chopped fresh flat-leaf parsley (optional)**

**Freshly ground black pepper, to taste**

| per 100g | MED fat | | LOW saturated fat | | MED salt | | LOW sugar | |
|---|---|---|---|---|---|---|---|---|
| per portion (% of GDA) | **181 kcal** 9% | **9.3g fat** 13% | **1.9g saturated fat** 10% | **0.9g salt** 15% | **5.5g sugars** 6% | | | |

# Baked potato skins with salmon & soft cheese

**Serves: 8 (makes 32 wedges)**
**Preparation time: 35 minutes**
**Cooking time: 1¼ hours**

**8 small baking potatoes (each about 200g/7oz), washed and dried**

**3 tablespoons olive oil**

**Freshly ground black pepper, to taste**

**115g (4oz) low-fat soft cheese (5% fat)**

**213g (7½oz) can red salmon in brine, drained and bones removed**

**1 teaspoon finely grated lemon zest**

**2 tablespoons snipped fresh chives**

*Crisp-baked potato skins can be topped with a soft cheese, salmon and chive mixture to make a nutritious and tasty snack that is ideal to serve at parties.*

1  Preheat the oven to 200°C/fan 180°C/gas mark 6. Brush the skins of the potatoes with 1 tablespoon of the olive oil. Place the potatoes on a non-stick baking sheet and bake for about 1 hour or until tender.

2  Remove the potatoes from the oven and cut them in half lengthways. Carefully scoop out the flesh, leaving a 1cm (½in) thick layer of potato next to the skin. Set the scooped flesh aside for another use. Cut each potato skin in half lengthways again and place them all, flesh-side up, in a single layer on a large, non-stick baking sheet.

3  Brush the flesh side of the potato skins with the remaining oil and season with black pepper, if desired. Return the potato skins to the oven and bake for a further 15–20 minutes or until golden and crisp. Meanwhile, put the soft cheese into a bowl. Flake the salmon and add it to the soft cheese together with the lemon zest, chives and black pepper, mixing well.

4  Remove the potato skins from the oven and allow to cool for 1–2 minutes. Top each potato skin with a spoonful of the salmon mixture, flattening the mixture slightly if desired. Serve immediately.

**Variation:** About 150g (5½oz) of cold poached fresh salmon fillet can be substituted for the canned salmon, if desired – you may need to add a little extra soft cheese and a squeeze or two of lemon juice to the poached salmon mixture.

| per 100g | MED **fat** | LOW **saturated fat** | LOW **salt** | LOW **sugar** |
|---|---|---|---|---|
| per portion (% of GDA) | **118 kcal** 6% **7.2g fat** 10% | **1.5g saturated fat** 7% | **0.2g salt** 3% | **0.9g sugars** 1% |

# Broad bean dip with vegetable crudités

**Serves: 2–3**
**Preparation time: 20 minutes**
**Cooking time: 5 minutes**

225g (8oz) frozen broad beans

40g (1½oz) low-fat soft cheese (5% fat)

1 tablespoon reduced-calorie mayonnaise

2 teaspoons finely chopped fresh mint

½ teaspoon finely grated lemon zest

Freshly ground black pepper, to taste

Selection of crudités, such as pepper, carrot and cucumber sticks, radishes, cherry tomatoes and baby sweetcorn

This is another great dish for entertaining, but is so healthy, you can eat it every day! Broad beans are low in fat and provide a vegetarian source of protein and fibre.

1  Cook the broad beans in a pan of boiling water for about 5 minutes or until tender. Drain well, refresh in cold water and drain again. Repeat the refreshing process once more. Now slip each bean out of its grey skin and discard the skins.

2  Mash the beans in a bowl, taking care to retain a little texture. Stir in the rest of the ingredients, mixing well.

3  Spoon the broad bean dip into a serving bowl and serve immediately with a selection of vegetable crudités.

**Variation:** Fresh (podded) broad beans can be substituted for the frozen broad beans – simply cook them in a pan of boiling water until tender.

**Cook's tip:** Ensure you do not mash the broad beans in their skins, but use only the shelled bean, which is the most tender part.

| per 100g | LOW fat | LOW saturated fat | LOW salt | LOW sugar |
|---|---|---|---|---|
| per portion (% of GDA) | 140 kcal 7% | 5g fat 7% | 1g saturated fat 5% | 0.2g salt 3% | 7g sugars 8% |

# Quick cheese & herb bread

**Serves: 6–8**
**Preparation time: 20 minutes**
**Cooking time: 25–35 minutes**

**140g (5oz) self-raising white flour**

**140g (5oz) self-raising wholemeal flour**

**1 teaspoon baking powder**

**55g (2oz) sunflower spread**

**115g (4oz) half-fat mature Cheddar-style cheese, finely grated**

**2–3 tablespoons chopped fresh mixed herbs, such as rosemary and flat-leaf parsley, plus extra for sprinkling**

**1 teaspoon mustard powder**

**A few turns of freshly ground black pepper**

**1 egg, beaten**

**About 150ml (¼ pint) skimmed milk**

**This tasty flavoured bread is quick and easy to make. Try serving it with one of the superb soups in this book for a satisfying lunch.**

1 Preheat the oven to 190°C/fan 170°C/gas mark 5. Flour or grease a non-stick baking sheet and set aside. Combine the flours and baking powder in a large bowl, then lightly rub in the sunflower spread until the mixture resembles breadcrumbs.

2 Stir in the cheese, herbs, mustard powder and black pepper. Add the egg and just enough milk to form a soft, but not too sticky, dough. Knead the dough gently on a lightly floured surface, then form it into a 17cm (6½in) round. Place this on the prepared baking sheet and, using a sharp knife, cut 3 slashes into the top of the loaf. Brush the top with milk and sprinkle with chopped fresh herbs.

3 Bake for 25–35 minutes or until the bread is cooked through and a deep golden brown on top. You'll know it is cooked if the loaf sounds hollow when tapped on the bottom. Transfer the loaf to a wire rack to cool. Serve warm or cold, in slices or wedges.

**Variation:** Try using 1½ teaspoons of dried herbes de Provence in place of the fresh herbs.

| per 100g | MED fat | MED saturated fat | MED salt | LOW sugar |
|---|---|---|---|---|
| per portion (% of GDA) | **213 kcal** 11% | **8.4g fat** 12% | **2.8g saturated fat** 14% | **0.4g salt** 7% | **1.6g sugars** 2% |

# Watercress soup

**Serves: 4**
**Preparation time: 15 minutes**
**Cooking time: 35 minutes**

**2 teaspoons sunflower oil**

**1 onion, chopped**

**1 leek, trimmed, washed and thinly sliced**

**1 large potato (about 225–250g/8–9oz peeled weight), peeled and diced**

**225g (8oz) watercress, roughly chopped**

**450ml (16fl oz) vegetable stock**

**450ml (16fl oz) semi-skimmed milk**

**Freshly ground black pepper or freshly grated nutmeg, to taste and garnish**

**This appetising soup is chock-full of goodness, and it looks and tastes great, too.**

1  Heat the sunflower oil in a large saucepan. Add the onion and leek and cook over a medium heat for 4–5 minutes or until softened, stirring occasionally. Add the potato and watercress and cook for a further 3 minutes or until the watercress wilts, stirring occasionally.

2  Stir in the stock and milk. Bring to the boil, then reduce the heat and simmer, covered, for about 20 minutes or until the potatoes are cooked and tender, stirring occasionally.

3  Remove the pan from the heat and allow the liquid to cool slightly. Purée the soup using a blender or food processor until smooth, then return the soup to the rinsed-out pan. (Alternatively, use a hand-held blender to carefully purée the soup in the pan until smooth.) Reheat the soup gently until hot, stirring occasionally. Season to taste with black pepper or nutmeg. Serve in warmed soup bowls with a sprinkling of coarsely ground black pepper or freshly grated nutmeg to garnish.

**Variations:** Try using chopped fresh spinach in place of watercress, if desired. 4 shallots can be substituted for the onion, if desired.

**To freeze:** To freeze, allow the puréed soup to cool completely, then transfer to a rigid freezer-proof container (freeze in individual portions, if desired). Cover, seal and label, and freeze for up to 3 months. To serve, defrost completely, then reheat gently in a saucepan until piping hot.

| per 100g | LOW fat | LOW saturated fat | LOW salt | LOW sugar |
|---|---|---|---|---|
| per portion (% of GDA) | **135 kcal** 8% | **4.6g fat** 7% | **1.6g saturated fat** 8% | **1g salt** 17% | **9.4g sugars** 10% |

# Mixed vegetable & bean soup

**Serves: 2**
**Preparation time: 15 minutes**
**Cooking time: 20 minutes**

**2 teaspoons olive oil**

**3 shallots, finely chopped**

**1 leek, trimmed, washed and thinly sliced**

**1 stick celery, chopped**

**1 tablespoon plain flour**

**450ml (16fl oz) vegetable stock (preferably homemade – see page 13)**

**1 teaspoon dried herbes de Provence**

**175g (6oz) frozen mixed vegetables, such as diced carrots, peas, cut green beans, sweetcorn kernels and broad beans**

**225g (8oz) canned red kidney beans, rinsed and drained**

**Freshly ground black pepper, to taste**

One portion of this hearty, nutritious soup is packed full of vegetables that will contribute towards your five-a-day. Served with fresh bread, this soup makes a tasty lunch or supper dish.

1  Heat the olive oil in a non-stick saucepan. Add the shallots, leek and celery and cook over a medium heat for about 5 minutes or until softened, stirring occasionally. Stir in the flour and cook gently for 1 minute, stirring.

2  Gradually stir in the stock. Bring to the boil, stirring. Stir in the herbs, frozen vegetables and kidney beans and season with black pepper. Bring back to the boil, then reduce the heat, cover and simmer for about 10 minutes or until the vegetables are cooked and tender, stirring occasionally. Ladle the soup into warmed bowls and serve with fresh bread, if desired.

**Variations:** 1 small onion can be substituted for the shallots, if desired. Try using a 210g (7½oz) can of chickpeas instead of the red kidney beans.

**Cook's tip:** Add a little extra hot stock (about 50ml/2fl oz) if you prefer a slightly thinner soup.

| per 100g | LOW fat | LOW saturated fat | MED salt | LOW sugar |
|---|---|---|---|---|
| per portion (% of GDA) | **225 kcal** 11% | **4.8g fat** 7% | **0.7g saturated fat** 4% | **1.6g salt** 27% | **10g sugars** 11% |

# Cumin-spiced parsnip soup

**Serves: 4–6**
**Preparation time: 15 minutes**
**Cooking time: 40 minutes**

2 teaspoons olive oil

1 large onion, chopped

1 clove garlic, crushed

3–4 sticks celery (about 175g/6oz total trimmed weight), chopped

1 tablespoon ground cumin

750g (1lb 10oz) parsnips (about 4 large parsnips), peeled and roughly chopped

1.2 litres (2 pints) vegetable stock

Freshly ground black pepper, to taste

Chopped fresh parsley or coriander, to garnish

**Parsnip, a great British winter vegetable, combines well with cumin in this inexpensive and easy-to-make dish, which is perfect for warming you up on a chilly winter day.**

1  Heat the olive oil in a large, non-stick saucepan. Add the onion, garlic and celery and cook gently for 5 minutes or until softened, stirring occasionally. Add the cumin and cook gently, stirring, for 1 minute to release its flavour.

2  Stir in the parsnips, stock and black pepper. Bring to the boil, then reduce the heat, cover and simmer for about 30 minutes or until the vegetables are tender, stirring occaisionally.

3  Remove the pan from the heat and cool slightly. Purée the soup until smooth using a blender or food processor, then return it to the rinsed-out pan. (Alternatively, use a hand-held blender to carefully purée the soup in the pan until smooth.) Reheat the soup gently until hot, stirring occasionally. Serve in wared soup bowls with a sprinkling of chopped herbs to garnish.

**Variation:** Use carrots in place of the parsnips. 1 large red onion can be substituted for the standard onion, if desired. Add an extra teaspoon of ground cumin for a slightly stronger spicy flavour.

**Cook's tip:** If you prefer a slightly thinner soup, stir in about 150ml (¼ pint) extra vegetable stock or semi-skimmed milk once the soup has been puréed and reheat gently until hot.

**To freeze:** Allow the puréed soup to cool completely, then transfer to a rigid freezer-proof container (freeze in individual portions, if desired). Cover, seal and label, and freeze for up to 3 months. To serve, defrost completely, then reheat gently in a saucepan until piping hot.

| per 100g | LOW fat | LOW saturated fat | LOW salt | LOW sugar |
|---|---|---|---|---|
| per portion (% of GDA) | **131 kcal** 7% | **5.3g fat** 8% | **0.8g saturated fat** 4% | **0.7g salt** 12% | **8.7g sugars** 10% |

# Pumpkin soup

Colourful and delicious, pumpkin soup is great for entertaining, as pretty much everyone likes it. If you've had a glut of pumpkins this year, making this dish is a wonderful way of using them up.

1   Heat the oil in a large non-stick saucepan. Add the onions, celery and garlic (if using) and cook over a medium-low heat for 5 minutes or until softened, stirring occasionally. Add the ground spices and cook gently for a further minute, stirring.

2   Stir in the pumpkin, stock and black pepper. Bring to the boil, then reduce the heat, cover and simmer for about 25 minutes or until the vegetables are tender, stirring occasionally.

3   Remove from the heat and allow to cool slightly. Purée the soup until smooth using a blender or food processor, then return it to the rinsed-out pan. (Alternatively, use a hand-held blender to carefully purée the soup in the pan until smooth.) Add up to 150ml (¼ pint) of extra stock if you prefer a thinner soup. Reheat gently until hot, stirring occasionally. Serve in warmed soup bowls, garnished with herb sprigs, with fresh crusty bread.

**Cook's tip:** Use your favourite herbs to garnish this soup. Fresh basil works well.

**To freeze:** Allow the soup to cool completely, then transfer to a rigid freezer-proof container. Cover, seal and label, and freeze for up to 3 months. To serve, defrost completely, then reheat gently in a saucepan until piping hot.

**Serves: 4**
**Preparation time: 15 minutes**
**Cooking time: 35 minutes**

**2 teaspoons sunflower oil**
**2 onions, chopped**
**2 sticks celery, chopped**
**1–2 cloves garlic, crushed (optional)**
**2 teaspoons ground coriander**
**2 teaspoons ground cumin**
**450g (1lb) pumpkin flesh (peeled and deseeded weight), diced**
**850ml (1½ pints) vegetable stock**
**Freshly ground black pepper, to taste**
**Fresh herb sprigs, to garnish**

| per 100g | LOW fat | | LOW saturated fat | | LOW salt | | LOW sugar | |
|---|---|---|---|---|---|---|---|---|
| per portion (% of GDA) | 113 kcal 6% | 6.7g fat 10% | 0.7g saturated fat 4% | | 0.5g salt 8% | | 6.5g sugars 7% | |

# Fish
## & SEAFOOD

# Baked citrus cod with fresh herbs

This tasty dish is quick and easy to make, super healthy and light, yet satisfying. The tangy dressing provides the perfect complement for the delicate flavour of cod – traditionally one of Britain's favourite fish.

**Serves: 2**
**Preparation time: 10 minutes**
**Cooking time: 20 minutes**

**Finely grated zest and juice of ½ lime**

**1 tablespoon freshly squeezed lemon juice (juice of about ½ small lemon)**

**2 teaspoons olive oil**

**1 teaspoon clear (runny) honey**

**1½ teaspoons chopped fresh tarragon**

**1½ teaspoons chopped fresh parsley**

**Freshly ground black pepper, to taste**

**2 cod steaks (about 175g/6oz each)**

1 Preheat the oven to 200°C/fan 180°C/gas mark 6. Put the lime zest and juice, lemon juice, oil, honey, chopped herbs and black pepper in a small bowl and whisk together until thoroughly mixed.

2 Place the cod steaks in an ovenproof dish and pour over the lime mixture. Cover the dish loosely with foil (ensure the foil does not touch the fish). Bake for 20 minutes or until the fish is cooked – the flesh should be tender and just beginning to flake. Serve with steamed carrots and green beans.

**Variation:** Substitute small halibut steaks for the cod steaks.

**Cook's tip:** Fish is a nutritious choice, but it's important that we consider the environment and sustainability issues when buying it. Look out for on-pack information or talk to your fishmonger to help guide you.

| per 100g | LOW fat | LOW saturated fat | LOW salt | LOW sugar |
|---|---|---|---|---|
| per portion (% of GDA) | **180 kcal** 9% | **4.5g fat** 6% | **0.5g saturated fat** 3% | **0.35g salt** 6% | **4.5g sugars** 5% |

# Fisherman's pie

**Serves: 6**
**Preparation time: 15–20 minutes**
**Cooking time: 50–55 minutes**

700g (1lb 9oz) potatoes, washed and chopped

300g (10½oz) skinless, boneless cod or haddock fillet

300g (10½oz) skinless salmon fillet

300ml (½ pint) semi-skimmed milk, plus a little extra for the mashed potato

2 bay leaves

25g (1oz) unsaturated margarine

2 small leeks, trimmed, washed and sliced

115g (4oz) mushrooms, wiped clean and sliced

25g (1oz) plain flour (white or wholemeal)

115g (4oz) frozen peas

2 tablespoons chopped fresh parsley

Freshly ground black pepper, to taste

Fresh parsley sprigs, to garnish (optional)

**Even people who think they don't like fish are converted when they taste this creamy classic dish. Just a few adjustments make it a very healthy meal for the whole family to enjoy.**

1   Preheat the oven to 190°C/fan 170°C/gas mark 5. Grease an ovenproof pie dish and set aside. Cook the potatoes in a saucepan of boiling water until tender, then drain well and set aside, keeping them hot.

2   Meanwhile, place the fish in a saucepan with the milk and bay leaves. Bring slowly to the boil, then poach the fish gently for 8–10 minutes or until the flesh is tender and flakes easily. Transfer the fish to a plate using a slotted spoon, flake the flesh and set aside. Strain the cooking liquid into a jug, discarding the bay leaves. Set aside.

3   Melt the margarine in a saucepan, add the leeks and mushrooms and sauté for 5 minutes. Add the flour and cook gently for 1 minute, stirring. Gradually add the reserved milk, stirring until the sauce is thickened and smooth. Simmer for 2 minutes, stirring.

4   Remove the pan from the heat and stir in the flaked fish, peas, chopped parsley and black pepper. Spoon the fish mixture into the prepared dish. Mash the potatoes with a little milk until soft and creamy and season to taste with black pepper. Pile or pipe the mashed potato on top of the fish mixture.

5   Bake for about 30 minutes or until golden brown and piping hot. Garnish the pie with parsley sprigs (if using), and serve with cooked vegetables, such as broccoli florets and baby carrots.

**Cook's tip:** Brush the top of the mash with beaten egg before baking for an extra-golden surface.

| per 100g | MED fat | LOW saturated fat | LOW salt | LOW sugar |
|---|---|---|---|---|
| per portion (% of GDA) | 307 kcal 15% | 10.9g fat 16% | 2.4g saturated fat 12% | 0.3g salt 5% | 4.3g sugars 5% |

# Salmon with warm tomato & herb dressing

**Serves: 4**
**Preparation time: 10 minutes**
**Cooking time: 25–30 minutes**

**200g (7oz) brown Basmati rice**
**4 x 150g (5½oz) skinless salmon fillets**
**Freshly ground black pepper, to taste**
**100g (3½oz) rocket, watercress or baby spinach**

**For the dressing:**
**4 vine-ripened tomatoes**
**Low-calorie cooking spray (or 1 teaspoon unsaturated oil)**
**1 large shallot, finely chopped**
**1 plump clove garlic, finely chopped**
**1–2 teaspoons red wine vinegar**
**1 teaspoon tarragon or 1 tablespoon basil, chopped**
**3 teaspoons extra virgin olive oil**

**Filling and flavoursome, this dish is perfect for a weekday supper. The rich dressing complements the tender flakes of salmon wonderfully.**

1  Cook the rice according to the instructions on the packet. Meanwhile, preheat the grill and line a baking tray with foil. Place the salmon fillets on the foil-lined tray and season with black pepper. Grill for 4–7 minutes or until cooked to your liking. Set aside, keeping them warm.

2  To skin the tomatoes, make a cross on the stalk ends with a sharp knife. Place the tomatoes in a bowl and cover with boiling water and, after 3–4 minutes, transfer them to a bowl of chilled water. Drain the tomatoes, then slip off their skins. Now quarter, deseed and finely chop them.

3  Mist a non-stick saucepan with cooking spray (or heat the oil in the pan) and lightly fry the shallot until just golden. Add the garlic and cook for a minute more. Stir in the tomatoes and their juices, along with the vinegar, herbs and olive oil to make a warm dressing. Add a dash more vinegar, if necessary, to suit your taste.

4  Prepare a bed of rocket, watercress or baby spinach on each plate. Place a cooked salmon fillet on each bed and serve with the rice alongside the fish and the dressing spooned over.

| per 100g | HIGH fat | LOW saturated fat | LOW salt | LOW sugar |
|---|---|---|---|---|
| per portion (% of GDA) | **493 kcal** 25% | **21.4g fat** 31% | **3.7g saturated fat** 19% | **0.3g salt** 5% | **4g sugars** 4% |

# Seared salmon with watercress sauce

**Serves: 2**
**Preparation time: 10 minutes**
**Cooking time: 10 minutes**

**2 salmon fillets (each about 140–175g/5–6oz), with skin left on**

**1 teaspoon olive oil**

**Watercress sprigs, to garnish**

**For the dressing:**

**140ml (5 fl oz) natural set bio yoghurt**

**25g (1oz) watercress, finely chopped**

**55g (2oz) cucumber, peeled, deseeded and finely chopped**

**1 teaspoon finely chopped fresh mint**

**Freshly ground black pepper, to taste**

**This delicious and simple supper supplies you with omega-3 fats from the salmon, which help to keep your heart healthy.**

1   First make the dressing. Put the yoghurt, watercress, cucumber, mint and black pepper in a bowl and stir gently to mix. Cover and chill while cooking the salmon.

2   Lightly brush the salmon fillets with olive oil and season with black pepper. Preheat a non-stick griddle or frying pan over a medium-high heat. Place the salmon fillets, skin-side down, in the pan and cook for 4–5 minutes or until the skin is crisp. Turn over the fillets and cook for a further 4–5 minutes or until the flesh is opaque and just beginning to flake.

3   Remove the skin from the salmon before serving, if desired. Serve the salmon fillets with watercress sauce spooned alongside and garnished with the watercress sprigs.

**Variations:** Try using tuna steaks instead of salmon fillets. 1 small clove of garlic, crushed, can be added to the yoghurt sauce.

**Cook's tip:** Choose fresh fish from sustainable sources where possible.

| per 100g | MED fat | LOW saturated fat | LOW salt | LOW sugar |
|---|---|---|---|---|
| per portion (% of GDA) | **341 kcal** 17% | **21g fat** 30% | **4g saturated fat** 20% | **0.5g salt** 8% | **6g sugars** 7% |

# Potato salad with flaked mackerel

**Potatoes and mackerel is a perfect combination of flavours and textures. Add the zing of orange zest and the peppery greens of watercress and you have a taste sensation that a TV chef would be proud to serve!**

1 Bring the potatoes to the boil in a pan of water and cook for 12–15 minutes, adding the green beans for the last 5 minutes, until both are tender. Drain well, refresh under cold running water and drain again thoroughly. Set aside to cool completely.

2 For the dressing, whisk together the oil, orange juice, vinegar, mustard, orange zest, chives and black pepper in a small bowl.

3 Put the cold potatoes and beans in a serving bowl. Add the watercress, spring onions and mackerel and toss gently. Give the dressing a whisk, then drizzle it over the salad. Toss gently again and serve.

**Serves: 2**
**Preparation time: 20 minutes, plus cooling time**
**Cooking time: 15 minutes**

**280g (10oz) waxy small salad potatoes**

**115g (4oz) green beans, trimmed**

**35g (1¼oz) small watercress sprigs**

**4 spring onions, finely chopped**

**125g (4½oz) can mackerel fillets in brine, rinsed, drained and flaked**

**For the dressing:**

**2 tablespoons olive oil**

**2 teaspoons unsweetened orange juice**

**1 teaspoon white wine vinegar**

**1 teaspoon wholegrain mustard, or to taste**

**¼ teaspoon finely grated orange zest**

**1 tablespoon snipped fresh chives**

**Freshly ground black pepper, to taste**

| per 100g | MED fat | | LOW saturated fat | | MED salt | | LOW sugar | |
|---|---|---|---|---|---|---|---|---|
| per portion (% of GDA) | **335 kcal** 17% | **19.5g fat** 28% | **4g saturated fat** 20% | | **1.35g salt** 23% | | **5g sugars** 6% | |

# Grilled mackerel with cherry tomato, pea & spinach salad

**Serves: 4**
**Preparation time: 10 minutes**
**Cooking time: 20 minutes**

500g (1lb 2oz) new potatoes

4 x 150g (5½oz) mackerel fillets

1 tablespoon coriander seeds, crushed

Freshly ground black pepper

Low-calorie cooking spray (or
    1 teaspoon unsaturated oil)

200g (7oz) frozen peas, defrosted

3 spring onions, finely sliced

250g (9oz) vine-ripened cherry
    tomatoes, halved

50g (1¾oz) baby spinach leaves

**For the dressing:**

1 teaspoon wholegrain mustard

1 teaspoon English mustard

1 teaspoon honey

2 teaspoons cider vinegar

4 teaspoons extra virgin olive oil

**A punchy dressing enhances the flavour of the grilled mackerel and the vegetables in this mouthwatering salad.**

1 Boil the potatoes for 12–15 minutes or until tender, then drain them. Halve or thickly slice them. Preheat the grill. Line a baking tray with foil.

2 Place the fish on the prepared baking tray, skin-side up, sprinkle with the crushed coriander seeds and season with black pepper. Mist with the cooking spray (or drizzle the oil over the fish), then grill, for 6–8 minutes, depending on the strength of your grill, until the flesh is opaque and the skin begins to blacken.

3 Make the dressing. In a bowl, mix together the mustards, honey, vinegar and oil. Now add the warm potatoes, peas, spring onions, tomatoes and spinach leaves. Divide the salad equally onto 4 plates, top with the cooked fish fillets and serve immediately.

| per 100g | HIGH fat | LOW saturated fat | LOW salt | LOW sugar |
|---|---|---|---|---|
| per portion (% of GDA) | 506 kcal 25% | 27.9g fat 40% | 5.5g saturated fat 28% | 0.5g salt 8% | 6.4g sugars 7% |

# Herrings with a peppercorn oatmeal crust

**Serves: 2**
**Preparation time: 10 minutes**
**Cooking time: 4–6 minutes**

25g (1oz) medium oatmeal

1 tablespoon chopped fresh flat-leaf parsley

1 teaspoon finely grated lemon zest

Freshly ground black pepper, to taste

2 whole fresh herrings (each about 225–250g/8–9oz unprepared weight), filleted

1½ teaspoons olive oil

Lemon wedges and watercress, to garnish

**While the added fat in this dish is low, it is high in fat due to the naturally occurring oil in the herrings. This oil is thought to be beneficial to heart health, so there's no reason why you can't enjoy this tasty dish.**

1 Cover a grill rack with foil and preheat the grill to medium-high. Combine the oatmeal, chopped parsley, lemon zest and black pepper in a small bowl and mix well.

2 Rinse the fish fillets and pat them dry. Smear the fleshy side of the fillets with olive oil and place them, flesh-side up, on the prepared rack in a grill pan. Sprinkle the oatmeal mixture evenly over the herring fillets and pat it down lightly.

3 Grill the fish fillets, placing them roughly 10cm (4in) away from the heat source, for 4–6 minutes without turning until they are cooked and the flesh flakes when tested with a fork.

4 Carefully transfer the fish fillets to warmed plates. Garnish with the lemon wedges and watercress and serve immediately, with thin slices of wholemeal bread, if desired.

**Variations:** Other oily fish, such as mackerel, can be substituted for the herrings. Try using orange or lime zest in place of the lemon zest. Try using a little extra lemon zest to garnish.

| per 100g | HIGH fat | MED saturated fat | MED salt | LOW sugar |
|---|---|---|---|---|
| per portion (% of GDA) | 341 kcal 17% | 24g fat 34% | 5.4g saturated fat 27% | 0.5g salt 8% | 0.4g sugars 0% |

# Meat

## DISHES

# Turkey, leek & bean bake

This dish is creamy, filling and satisfying – yet lean and healthy. Turkey is a good source of protein without too much fat, so make this a regular on your weekly menu.

1 Preheat the oven to 200°C/fan 180°C/gas mark 6, then lightly grease an 850ml–1.2 litre (1½–2 pint) ovenproof dish. Steam the leeks and mushrooms with the bouquet garni over a pan of gently boiling water for about 10 minutes or until just tender. Remove from the heat and discard the bouquet garni. Drain the vegetables well and set aside.

2 Place the sunflower spread, flour and milk in a saucepan. Heat gently, whisking, until the sauce comes to the boil and is thickened and smooth. Simmer gently for 2 minutes, stirring. Stir in the mustard, 2 tablespoons of the herbs and black pepper to taste. Then stir in the cooked vegetables, turkey and beans.

3 Spoon the mixture into the prepared ovenproof dish. Combine the mashed potato, the remaining herbs, some black pepper and a dash of extra milk and mix well. Spoon the mash on top of the turkey mixture, covering it completely. Bake for about 25 minutes, or until the topping is golden brown. Serve with cooked green vegetables.

**Serves: 3–4**
**Preparation time: 30 minutes**
**Cooking time: 25 minutes**

- **2 medium leeks, trimmed, washed and sliced**
- **85g (3oz) button mushrooms, wiped clean and sliced**
- **1 bouquet garni**
- **15g (½oz) sunflower spread**
- **15g (½oz) plain flour**
- **200ml (7fl oz) semi-skimmed milk, plus a dash for the mashed potato**
- **1 teaspoon Dijon mustard**
- **3 tablespoons snipped fresh chives or parsley**
- **Freshly ground black pepper, to taste**
- **115g (4oz) cooked skinless, boneless turkey, diced**
- **115g (4oz) canned beans (rinsed and drained weight), such as borlotti, flageolet or red kidney beans**
- **280g (10oz) cold, cooked mashed potato**

| per 100g | MED fat | LOW saturated fat | LOW salt | LOW sugar |
|---|---|---|---|---|
| per portion (% of GDA) | 214 kcal 11% | 7.7g fat 11% | 2g saturated fat 10% | 0.7g salt 11% | 5.4g sugars 6% |

# Roast chicken with hazelnut & orange stuffing

**Serves: 4–6**
**Preparation time: 30 minutes**
**Cooking time: about 2 hours**

**1 free range chicken (about 1.5kg/ 3lb 5oz unprepared weight)**

**150ml (¼ pint) well-flavoured chicken or vegetable stock**

**150ml (¼ pint) fresh orange juice**

**1 teaspoon plain flour**

**For the stuffing:**

**200g (7oz) onion, diced**

**300g (10½oz) butternut squash, roughly diced**

**110g (3¾oz) hazelnuts, roughly chopped**

**2 sprigs fresh rosemary**

**1 teaspoon olive oil**

**Freshly ground black pepper**

**115g (4oz) brown Basmati rice**

**Grated zest and juice of 1 large orange, and the squeezed-out orange halves, plus 1 orange, cut into wedges (optional)**

**1 tablespoon chopped fresh parsley**

**A good roast chicken is the perfect family meal. Serve this heart-healthy version with broccoli florets mixed with peas.**

1 Make the stuffing. Preheat the oven to 200°C/fan 180°C/gas mark 6. Tip the onion, squash, hazelnuts and rosemary into a shallow roasting tin and drizzle over the oil. Mix together and season with plenty of pepper. Roast for 15–20 minutes, stirring occasionally, until beginning to turn golden brown.

2 Meanwhile, cook the Basmati rice in plenty of boiling water for about 20–25 minutes until just tender. Drain well and rinse with cold water to cool.

3 Remove the rosemary sprigs from the roasted ingredients and stir in the rice with the orange zest and juice. Leave to cool. Reduce the oven temperature to 190°C/fan 170°C/gas mark 5. Spoon a little stuffing into the neck end of the chicken, folding under the loose flap of skin to hold the stuffing in place. Place the squeezed orange halves into the larger cavity of the chicken and put the bird in a roasting tin just large enough to hold it. Spoon the remaining stuffing into a small ovenproof dish and cover with foil. Set aside.

4 Pour the stock around the chicken, pop in the orange wedges (if using) and roast for 1¼–1½ hours until golden and tender, basting occasionally. Add the stuffing for the last 30 minutes. Transfer the chicken to a large plate. Reserve the cooking juices. Cover with foil and leave for 10 minutes before carving.

5 To make the gravy, set the roasting tin over a medium heat. Pour in the orange juice. Mix the flour to a paste with 2 teaspoons of cold water and whisk into the liquid. Bring to the boil, whisking, and allow the liquid to bubble until thickened. Remove from the heat, season and keep warm.

6 Stir the chopped parsley into the extra stuffing before serving.

| per 100g | MED fat | LOW saturated fat | LOW salt | LOW sugar |
|---|---|---|---|---|
| per portion (% of GDA) | **455 kcal** 23% | **20.4g fat** 30% | **3.3g saturated fat** 17% | **0.3g salt** 5% | **7.9g sugars** 9% |

# Chilli con carne

**Serves: 4**
**Preparation time: 20 minutes**
**Cooking time: 1 hour**

2 teaspoons sunflower oil

1 large red onion, chopped

2 carrots, peeled and finely chopped

2 sticks celery or 2 courgettes, finely chopped

1–2 cloves garlic, crushed

2 fresh red chillies, deseeded (if desired) and finely chopped

350g (12oz) extra-lean minced beef (5% fat)

1 teaspoon each hot chilli powder, ground cumin and ground coriander

2 teaspoons tomato purée

1½ teaspoons dark soft brown sugar

400g (14oz) can chopped tomatoes

250ml (9fl oz) homemade vegetable stock (see page 13)

400g (14oz) can red kidney beans in water, rinsed and drained

Chopped fresh coriander, to garnish (optional)

While this is not a traditional British recipe, it is certainly one that has become part of the modern cuisine of the nation. This healthier take on a hugely popular dish is sure to satisfy even the most ardent of chilli eaters.

1   Heat the oil in a heavy based non-stick saucepan, then add the onion, carrots, celery, garlic and chillies. Cook over a medium heat for 10 minutes or until the vegetables are beginning to soften, stirring occasionally.

2   Add the minced beef and cook for about 10 minutes or until the beef is coloured all over, stirring regularly and breaking up the meat.

3   Stir in the ground spices and tomato purée and cook for 1 minute, stirring. Add the sugar, tomatoes and stock. Bring to the boil, reduce the heat, cover and simmer gently for 30 minutes, stirring occasionally.

4   Stir in the kidney beans, increase the heat slightly and cook gently for a further 10–15 minutes. Remove from the heat and garnish with the chopped coriander, if desired. Serve hot with cooked rice.

| per 100g | LOW fat | LOW saturated fat | LOW salt | LOW sugar |
|---|---|---|---|---|
| per portion (% of GDA) | **333 kcal** 17% | **11.3g fat** 16% | **4g saturated fat** 20% | **0.5g salt** 8% | **11.2g sugars** 12% |

# Spaghetti bolognese

The Italians invented it but the British have claimed it as a firm family favourite. This tasty version provides a healthy option for those who love their "Spag-bol".

**Serves: 6**
**Preparation time: 10 minutes**
**Cooking time: 1 hour 40 minutes**

**500g (1lb 2oz) extra-lean minced beef**

**1 onion, chopped**

**1 clove garlic, crushed**

**2 carrots, peeled and finely chopped**

**175g (6oz) mushrooms, wiped clean and finely chopped**

**3 sticks celery, finely chopped**

**400g (14oz) can chopped tomatoes**

**2 tablespoons tomato purée**

**2 teaspoons dried Italian herb seasoning or dried mixed herbs**

**300ml (½ pint) homemade beef stock**

**150ml (¼ pint) red wine**

**Freshly ground black pepper, to taste**

**400g (14oz) dried spaghetti (white or wholemeal)**

**Chopped fresh parsley, to garnish**

1  Place the minced beef, onion and garlic in a large saucepan and cook gently, stirring occasionally, until the mince is lightly browned all over.

2  Add the carrots, mushrooms and celery to the pan and cook for 5 minutes. Stir in the tomatoes, tomato purée, dried herbs, stock, wine and black pepper. Bring to the boil, then reduce the heat, cover and simmer for 1 hour.

3  Uncover the pan, increase the heat slightly and simmer for 20–30 minutes to thicken the sauce, stirring occasionally.

4  Meanwhile, cook the spaghetti in a large saucepan of boiling water until the pasta is just cooked or *al dente*. Drain thoroughly.

5  Pile the cooked spaghetti onto warmed serving plates and spoon the bolognese sauce over the top. Garnish with chopped parsley and serve with a mixed green salad.

**Cook's tip:** Use homemade beef stock in place of red wine, if desired.

| per 100g | LOW fat | | LOW saturated fat | | LOW salt | | LOW sugar | |
|---|---|---|---|---|---|---|---|---|
| per portion (% of GDA) | **391 kcal** 20% | **5.6g fat** 8% | **1.8g saturated fat** 9% | | **0.4g salt** 7% | | **8.4g sugars** 9% | |

# Spiced beef & carrot burgers

**Serves: 4 (makes 8 medium burgers)**
**Preparation time: 20 minutes**
**Cooking time: 20 minutes**

**450g (1lb) good-quality lean or extra-lean minced beef**

**2 small carrots (about 140g/5oz total unprepared weight), coarsely grated**

**85g (3oz) mushrooms, wiped clean and finely chopped**

**1 onion, finely chopped**

**55g (2oz) fresh wholemeal or white breadcrumbs**

**2 tablespoons tomato purée**

**1 egg, lightly beaten**

**1 clove garlic, crushed**

**2 teaspoons ground cumin**

**2 teaspoons ground coriander**

**1 teaspoon hot chilli powder**

**Freshly ground black pepper, to taste**

These healthy burgers will be a real hit with all the family. The carrot gives them a good moist texture. Try serving them in wholemeal or granary baps piled high with crisp salad leaves, tomato and red onion slices, and topped with a tangy relish.

1 Preheat the grill to medium. Place all the ingredients in a large bowl and mix together well.

2 Using your hands, shape the mixture into 8 round flat burgers, each about 1.5cm (½in) thick.

3 Place the patties on a rack in a grill pan and grill for about 20 minutes until the burgers are cooked to your liking, turning once or twice. (Don't grill the burgers too close to the heat – position them about 8cm/3¼in away from the heat source.) Serve in baps with salad and relish.

**Variations:** Substitute lean minced pork or lamb for the minced beef. Use 1 courgette in place of the carrots.

**To freeze:** Make the burgers as directed in step 2 and freeze them before cooking. Wrap them individually, label and freeze for up to 1 month. To serve, defrost completely, then grill as directed in step 3.

| per 100g | MED fat | MED saturated fat | LOW salt | LOW sugar |
|---|---|---|---|---|
| per portion (% of GDA) | **283 kcal** 14% | **13.6g fat** 19% | **5.6g saturated fat** 28% | **0.6g salt** 10% | **6.9g sugars** 8% |

# Puddings
## & BAKES

# Raspberry yoghurt ice

The perfect alternative to ice cream, this tempting dessert is very quick and easy to put together, although it does require some time for freezing and chilling. It's ideal for entertaining – even children love it!

1 Put the raspberries into the bowl of a blender or food processor and blend until smooth. Press the raspberry purée through a nylon sieve into a bowl and discard the pips. Add the sugar and mix well.

2 Stir in both types of yoghurt, mixing well. Pour the mixture into a shallow, freezer-proof container, cover and freeze for 2 hours. Meanwhile, put a clean, empty bowl into the refrigerator to chill.

3 Spoon the raspberry mixture into the chilled bowl. Now beat it with a fork or whisk it until it is smooth to break down the ice crystals. Return the mixture to the container, cover and freeze for a further 3–4 hours or until firm.

4 Transfer the yoghurt ice to the refrigerator for about 30 minutes before serving to soften. Serve decorated with the mint and raspberries, if desired.

**Variation:** Ripe fresh strawberries and low-fat strawberry yoghurt can be substituted for the raspberries and raspberry yoghurt.

**Serves: 4–6**
**Preparation time: 15 minutes, plus freezing and chilling time**
**Cooking time: none**

350g (12oz) ripe sweet fresh raspberries

55g (2oz) caster sugar

2 x 150g (5½oz) pots low-fat raspberry yoghurt

115ml (4fl oz) virtually fat-free natural Greek-style yoghurt

Fresh mint sprigs and additional raspberries, to decorate (optional)

| per 100g | LOW fat | | LOW saturated fat | | LOW salt | | MED sugar | |
|---|---|---|---|---|---|---|---|---|
| per portion (% of GDA) | **104 kcal** 5% | **0.6g fat** 1% | **0.3g saturated fat** 2% | **0.12g salt** 2% | **22g sugars** 24% | | | |

# Summer pudding

**Serves: 4**
**Preparation time: 15 minutes, plus chilling time**
**Cooking time: 5 minutes**

**225g (8oz) fresh or frozen mixed summer berries, such as raspberries, loganberries, blackcurrants and redcurrants**

**150ml (¼ pint) water**

**Caster sugar, to taste**

**4–6 medium slices bread from a large loaf (white or wholemeal), crusts removed**

**Fresh redcurrant sprigs and fresh raspberries, to decorate**

**A modern take on a traditional British pudding; low in fat, yet it still feels like a very special summertime treat.**

1 Put the fruit into a saucepan, add the water, cover and cook gently until the fruit is tender. Remove the pan from the heat and add just enough sugar to sweeten the fruit.

2 Reserve 1 slice of bread. Cut the remaining bread slices into fingers and use about ⅔ of the bread fingers to line a 600ml (1 pint) pudding basin.

3 Half-fill the bread-lined basin with half of the fruit and top with a layer of the remaining bread fingers. Spoon the remaining fruit into a basin and top this with a lid of bread using the reserved slice of bread, shaped to fit.

4 Pour over any remaining fruit juices and cover with a plate that just fits inside the basin. Place a weight on top of the plate, allow to cool, then chill for several hours or overnight before serving.

5 Carefully unmould the pudding onto a serving plate and decorate with redcurrant sprigs and raspberries. Serve with low-fat custard or fromage frais.

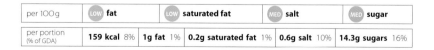

| per 100g | LOW fat | LOW saturated fat | MED salt | MED sugar |
|---|---|---|---|---|
| per portion (% of GDA) | **159 kcal** 8% | **1g fat** 1% · **0.2g saturated fat** 1% | **0.6g salt** 10% | **14.3g sugars** 16% |

# Blackberry yoghurt fool

**Serves: 2**
**Preparation time: 15 minutes, plus chilling time**
**Cooking time: none**

**225g (8oz) fresh ripe blackberries**

**1–2 tablespoons clear (runny) honey, or to taste**

**100ml (3½fl oz) thick low-fat plain yoghurt**

**2 tablespoons reduced-fat crème fraîche**

**This refreshing fruit fool is easy to prepare and makes the most of freshly foraged hedgerow blackberries.**

1 Put the blackberries into the bowl of a blender or food processor and blend until smooth. Press the purée through a sieve into a bowl and discard the seeds. (Alternatively, thoroughly mash the blackberries in a bowl, then press the purée through a sieve as above.)

2 Add the honey to the blackberry purée and mix well. Gently fold in the yoghurt and crème fraîche until combined.

3 Spoon the mixture into serving glasses or dishes and chill before serving. Serve with sponge fingers or oat biscuits.

**Variations:** Use mixed fresh berries, such as strawberries, raspberries and blueberries, in place of the blackberries. Use the same quantity of peeled, stoned ripe mango flesh instead of the blackberries, if desired.

**Cook's tip:** For a blackberry custard fool, purée and sieve the blackberries as above. Fold in 100ml (3½fl oz) of ready-made cold low-fat custard instead of the yoghurt, then fold in the crème fraîche. Add 1 tablespoon of honey. Serve chilled.

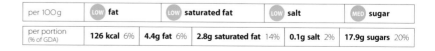

| per 100g | LOW fat | LOW saturated fat | LOW salt | MED sugar |
|---|---|---|---|---|
| per portion (% of GDA) | **126 kcal** 6% | **4.4g fat** 6% | **2.8g saturated fat** 14% | **0.1g salt** 2% | **17.9g sugars** 20% |

# Summer berry brulée

Serves: **2**
Preparation time: **10 minutes, plus**
**25 minutes' standing time**
Cooking time: **2–3 minutes**

**175g (6oz) mixed summer berries, such as raspberries, strawberries and blueberries**

**1½ teaspoons unsweetened apple juice**

**1½ teaspoons clear (runny) honey, or to taste**

**85ml (3fl oz) natural yoghurt**

**115ml (4fl oz) reduced-fat natural Greek-style yoghurt**

**35g (1¼oz) light soft brown sugar**

**Try this tasty lower fat version of a classic dessert.**

1 Put the mixed berries in a bowl and lightly crush the fruit with a fork. Add the apple juice and honey and stir to mix. Set aside for 20 minutes.

2 Spoon the berry mixture into 2 ovenproof ramekins or small ovenproof dishes, dividing it equally. Put the yoghurts into a bowl and fold together to mix, then spoon the yoghurt over the berry mixture and spread evenly.

3 Preheat the grill to high. Sprinkle the sugar evenly over the yoghurt. Place the dishes under a hot grill (close to the heat source) and grill for 2–3 minutes or until the sugar has melted and is bubbling and caramelised. Remove from the grill and leave to stand for 5 minutes before serving. Do not chill, as the caramel topping will become soft.

| per 100g | LOW fat | LOW saturated fat | LOW salt | HIGH sugar |
|---|---|---|---|---|
| per portion (% of GDA) | **184 kcal** 9% | **2.3g fat** 3% | **1.3g saturated fat** 7% | **0.2g salt** 3% | **36g sugars** 40% |

# Hot spiced pears

**Serves: 2**
**Preparation time: 10 minutes**
**Cooking time: 50 minutes to 1 hour 5 minutes**

2 large Conference pears (each about 225g/8oz unprepared weight)

150ml (¼ pint) red wine

4 tablespoons unsweetened orange juice

35g (1¼oz) light soft brown sugar

1 cinnamon stick, broken in half

2 star anise

Finely pared orange zest, to decorate (optional)

Quintessentially British, the pear is excellent in desserts, and combines beautifully with the flavours of cinnamon and star anise. This impressive-looking low-fat dessert is special enough to serve at dinner parties.

1 Preheat the oven to 180°C/fan 160°C/gas mark 4. Carefully peel the pears, leaving the stalks intact and the fruit whole. Place the pears in an ovenproof dish, laying them on their sides.

2 Combine the red wine, orange juice and sugar in a small saucepan. Heat gently, stirring, until the sugar has dissolved, then bring to the boil. Tuck the whole spices around the pears in the ovenproof dish, then pour the hot wine mixture over the pears and turn them over in the liquid a couple of times. Cover the dish and bake for 45 minutes to 1 hour or until the pears are soft, turning them once or twice during cooking.

3 Carefully lift out the pears with a slotted spoon and place them upright on serving dishes. Pour the liquid back into the saucepan and discard the whole spices. Bring the liquid to the boil and boil rapidly for 5 minutes or until it has reduced and thickened slightly. Spoon the liquid over the pears, dividing it equally between each dish. Decorate the pears with orange zest, if desired. Serve hot or warm, or cool and chill before serving.

**Variation:** Try using other large dessert pears, such as Packham pears, in place of the Conference pears.

| per 100g | LOW fat | LOW saturated fat | LOW salt | HIGH sugar |
|---|---|---|---|---|
| per portion (% of GDA) | **244 kcal** 11% | **0.25g fat** 0% | **0g saturated fat** 0% | **0.05g salt** 1% | **44g sugars** 49% |

# Fruity rice pudding

Rice pudding is a traditional dish that can be traced back to Tudor times. Fruity and full of goodness, this feel-good recipe is easy to digest and very comforting to eat.

**Serves: 2**
**Preparation time: 5 minutes**
**Cooking time: 35–40 minutes**

**160g (5¾oz) fresh strawberries**
**20g (¾oz) soft brown sugar**
**50g (1¾oz) pudding rice**
**380ml (13fl oz) semi-skimmed milk**
**¼ teaspoon vanilla extract**

1  Preheat the oven to 200°C/fan 180°C/gas mark 6. Wash and hull the strawberries, then chop them into large chunks and transfer to a bowl. Sprinkle over half of the sugar and set aside to allow the sugar to soak into the fruit.

2  Put the rice, milk, vanilla extract and the remaining sugar in a saucepan and stir well. Bring to the boil, stirring the rice to ensure it doesn't stick to the bottom of the pan. Then reduce the heat and simmer gently for 15 minutes or until the rice has absorbed most of the milk and is cooked. Stir the rice occasionally to stop it sticking.

3  At the end of the cooking time, mix in the strawberries and any juices they have made.

4  Transfer the rice pudding to individual baking dishes, set these on a baking tray and bake for another 20 minutes or until a golden brown skin forms.

| per 100g | LOW fat | LOW saturated fat | LOW salt | HIGH sugar |
|---|---|---|---|---|
| per portion (% of GDA) | **231 kcal** 12% | **3.7g fat** 5% | **2.1g saturated fat** 11% | **0.3g salt** 5% | **23g sugars** 26% |

# Apple & raspberry oatmeal crumble

**Serves: 6**
**Preparation time: 10 minutes**
**Cooking time: 45 minutes**

**85g (3oz) plain flour (white or wholemeal)**

**55g (2oz) medium oatmeal**

**55g (2oz) unsaturated margarine**

**70g (2½ oz) light soft brown sugar**

**1 teaspoon ground cinnamon**

**3 dessert apples, peeled, cored and thinly sliced**

**225g (8oz) fresh raspberries**

**2 tablespoons unsweetened apple juice**

**1 tablespoon clear (runny) honey**

The crumble is one of Britain's great inventions, and this lower fat version uses oatmeal, which has many health benefits. Oatmeal contains soluble fibre, which may help to reduce cholesterol.

1 Preheat the oven to 180°C/fan 160°C/gas mark 4. Put the flour and oatmeal in a bowl and stir to mix. Lightly rub in the margarine until the mixture resembles breadcrumbs. Stir in the sugar and cinnamon.

2 Place the apples and raspberries in an ovenproof dish. Mix together the apple juice and honey, pour this over the fruit and stir gently to mix. Spoon the crumble mixture evenly over the fruit to completely cover it.

3 Bake for 45 minutes or until golden brown. Serve hot or cold with low-fat custard or ice cream.

**Variations:** Use fresh blueberries in place of the raspberries. Use dessert pears in place of the apples. Use ground mixed spice or ginger in place of the cinnamon. Make individual portions by dividing the ingredients equally between 6 mini-pudding basins. Cook for 20–25 minutes.

| per 100g | MED fat | LOW saturated fat | LOW salt | MED sugar |
|---|---|---|---|---|
| per portion (% of GDA) | **246 kcal** 12% | **8.7g fat** 12% | **1.7g saturated fat** 9% | **0.2g salt** 3% | **24.6g sugars** 27% |

# Peach & apricot sponge pudding

**Serves: 4–6**
**Preparation time: 20 minutes**
**Cooking time: 1¼ hours**

**2 tablespoons golden syrup**

**40g (1½oz) ready-to-eat dried peaches, chopped**

**40g (1½oz) ready-to-eat dried apricots, chopped**

**85g (3oz) sunflower spread**

**85g (3oz) caster sugar**

**1 large egg**

**115g (4oz) self-raising flour, sifted**

**4 teaspoons semi-skimmed milk**

**Few drops vanilla extract**

The delicate yet intense flavours of apricots and peaches combine very pleasingly in this fragrant and delicious sponge pudding.

1 Lightly grease an 850ml (1½ pint) pudding basin. Spoon the golden syrup into the base of the prepared basin. Combine the dried fruit and scatter it on top of the syrup. Set aside.

2 Put the sunflower spread, sugar, egg, flour, milk and vanilla extract in a bowl and beat together until thoroughly mixed. Spoon the mixture over the fruit in the basin, spreading evenly. Cover the basin with a double layer of pleated non-stick baking paper and secure this in place with string.

3 Put the basin in the top half of a steamer placed over a pan of boiling water and cover. Steam for about 1¼ hours or until the pudding has risen and is cooked. Top up the boiling water as necessary during the cooking time.

4 Remove the basin from the steamer and carefully remove the cover. Loosen the pudding around the edges with a round-bladed knife and turn it out onto a warmed serving plate. Serve hot, cut into wedges, with low-fat custard, if desired.

**Variations:** Other ready-to-eat dried fruits, such as pears, sultanas or dates, can be substituted for the peaches or apricots. Try using a little finely grated lemon or orange zest in place of the vanilla extract.

**Cook's tip:** Cool any leftover sponge pudding, wrap it and keep it in a cool place. Serve warm (reheated) or cold the next day.

| per 100g | MED fat | MED saturated fat | MED salt | HIGH sugar |
|---|---|---|---|---|
| per portion (% of GDA) | 281 kcal 14% | 13g fat 19% · 2.7g saturated fat 14% | 0.4g salt 7% | 26g sugars 29% |

# Spiced apple bread pudding

This healthy take on a traditional British nursery pudding combines the flavours of apples and apricots with a little spice for added interest.

1  Lightly grease a shallow ovenproof dish. Thinly spread one side of each bread slice with the sunflower spread, then the jam. Cut the bread into triangles and arrange half of these in the dish, jam-side up.

2  Mix together the apple slices, mixed spice and half of the sugar. Spoon this apple mixture evenly over the bread, then arrange the remaining bread triangles over the top, jam-side up. Sprinkle evenly with the remaining sugar.

3  Beat together the egg and milk in a bowl or jug and pour the mixture evenly over the bread. Set aside for 30 minutes to allow the bread to absorb some of the liquid.

4  Preheat the oven to 180°C/fan 160°C/gas mark 4. Bake the bread pudding for 35–40 minutes or until lightly set and golden brown. Serve hot.

**Variations:** Ground cinnamon or ginger can be substituted for the mixed spice. Try using a dessert pear in place of the apple. Fine-shred orange marmalade can be substituted for the apricot jam.

**Serves: 4**
**Preparation time: 20 minutes, plus standing time**
**Cooking time: 35–40 minutes**

**3 medium slices bread**
**15g (½ oz) reduced-fat sunflower spread**
**25g (1 oz) apricot jam**
**1 dessert apple (about 150g/5½oz unprepared weight), peeled, cored and sliced**
**½ teaspoon ground mixed spice**
**25g (1oz) light soft brown sugar**
**1 egg**
**300ml (½ pint) semi-skimmed milk**

| per 100g | MED fat | LOW saturated fat | MED salt | MED sugar | |
|---|---|---|---|---|---|
| per portion (% of GDA) | **190 kcal** 10% | **5g fat** 7% | **1.7g saturated fat** 9% | **0.6g salt** 10% | **19.5g sugars** 22% |

# Lemon & raspberry roulade

**Serves: 6–8**
**Preparation time:** **25 minutes, plus cooling time**
**Cooking time: 8–10 minutes**

**4 large eggs**
**115g (4oz) caster sugar**
**Finely grated zest of 1 lemon**
**115g (4oz) plain flour, sifted**
**115ml (4fl oz) natural Greek-style yoghurt**
**115g (4oz) virtually fat-free natural fromage frais**
**2 tablespoons luxury lemon curd**
**175g (6oz) fresh raspberries**
**Sifted icing sugar, for dusting**

While not British in origin, the rolled dessert has been absorbed into British culinary tradition – think of the ubiquitous Swiss roll, or the chocolate log that graces many a Christmas table. This light and refreshing summertime version is perfect for parties.

1   Preheat the oven to 200°C/fan 180°C/gas mark 6. Grease a 33cm x 23cm (13in x 9in) Swiss roll tin and line it with non-stick baking paper. Put the eggs and caster sugar in a heatproof bowl set over a pan of simmering water. Using a hand-held electric whisk, whisk for about 5 minutes or until pale, thick and creamy. Remove the pan from the heat and whisk for a further 1–2 minutes or until cool.

2   Lightly fold in the lemon zest, flour and 1 tablespoon of hot water using a metal spoon. Pour the mixture evenly into the prepared tin and bake for 8–10 minutes or until risen and golden brown.

3   Invert the sponge onto a sheet of non-stick baking paper, quickly trim off the edges with a sharp knife and roll up the cake loosely, using the paper to help you roll. Place the roll, seam-side down, on a wire rack to cool.

4   Mix the yoghurt, fromage frais and lemon curd. Carefully unroll the sponge and spread the mixture over the cake. Scatter over the raspberries and roll up again. Dust with icing sugar to serve.

**Cook's tip:** Dust the roulade with caster sugar instead of icing sugar, if you prefer.

| per 100g | MED fat | LOW saturated fat | LOW salt | HIGH sugar |
|---|---|---|---|---|
| per portion (% of GDA) | **196 kcal** 10% | **5g fat** 7% | **1.7g saturated fat** 9% | **0.3g salt** 5% | **18.9g sugars** 21% |

# Lemon layer pudding

**Serves: 4–6**
**Preparation time: 20 minutes**
**Cooking time: 40 minutes**

**55g (2oz) sunflower spread**
**115g (4oz) caster sugar**
**Finely grated zest and juice of
1 large lemon**
**2 eggs, separated**
**55g (2oz) self-raising flour, sifted**
**300ml (½ pint) semi-skimmed milk**

**This sweet treat is easy to make and simply delicious. The pudding separates during cooking, creating a light spongy top with a luxurious lemon sauce underneath.**

1 Preheat the oven to 180°C/fan 160°C/gas mark 4. Lightly grease an ovenproof dish and set aside. Put the sunflower spread, sugar, lemon zest and juice, egg yolks and flour in a bowl and beat or whisk together until thoroughly mixed. Add the milk and beat again until well mixed.

2 In a separate bowl, whisk the egg whites until stiff, then fold carefully into the lemon mixture. Transfer the mixture to the prepared dish. Place this in a shallow roasting tin and pour enough hot water into the tin to reach halfway up the sides of dish.

3 Bake for 40 minutes or until the top is golden brown and spongy to the touch. Serve immediately.

| per 100g | MED fat | MED saturated fat | LOW salt | HIGH sugar |
|---|---|---|---|---|
| per portion (% of GDA) | **223 kcal** 11% | **10g fat** 14% | **2.5g saturated fat** 13% | **0.3g salt** 5% | **23g sugars** 6% |

# Plum batter dessert

If you are looking for a good way to use up a glut of plums, look no further. But if you don't grow you own, there are many varieties available, and this delicious dessert, which is low in both fat and sugar, can be made with any dessert plum.

1 Preheat the oven to 220°C/fan 200°C/gas mark 7. Combine the flour, caster sugar and cinnamon in a bowl. Make a well in the centre of the flour mixture and break the egg into this. Add a little milk and beat thoroughly with a wooden spoon. Gradually beat in the remaining milk, drawing in flour from the sides of the bowl to make a smooth batter.

2 Put the oil in a shallow 18cm (7in) square non-stick cake tin. Heat this in the oven for 2–3 minutes or until hot. Quickly and carefully place the plum halves, cut-sides down, over the base of the tin (the hot oil may spit slightly, so be careful). Pour the batter evenly over the fruit and bake for 25 minutes or until the pudding is cooked, risen and nicely browned. Dust with sifted icing sugar, if desired. Cut into portions and serve.

**Variations:** Ground mixed spice or ginger can be substituted for the cinnamon. Try using 3–4 fresh apricots in place of the plums.

**Cook's tip:** This pudding is also tasty served cold (cool any leftovers, then refrigerate and enjoy the next day).

**Serves: 4**
**Preparation time: 15 minutes**
**Cooking time: 25 minutes**

**55g (2oz) plain wholemeal flour**

**25g (1oz) caster sugar**

**½ teaspoon ground cinnamon**

**1 egg**

**125ml (4fl oz) semi-skimmed milk**

**1½ teaspoons sunflower oil**

**3–4 ripe, sweet red dessert plums, such as Splendor (about 300g/10½oz total unprepared weight), halved and stoned**

**Icing sugar, for dusting (optional)**

| per 100g | LOW fat | | LOW saturated fat | | LOW salt | | LOW sugar | |
|---|---|---|---|---|---|---|---|---|
| per portion (% of GDA) | **141 kcal** 7% | **3.8g fat** 5% | **0.9g saturated fat** 5% | **0.1g salt** 2% | **14.5g sugars** 16% | | | |

# Fresh strawberry scones

**Serves: 4**
**Preparation time: 15 minutes**
**Cooking time: 10–12 minutes**

**115g (4oz) self-raising wholemeal flour, plus extra for dusting**

**½ teaspoon baking powder**

**½ teaspoon ground cinnamon**

**25g (1oz) sunflower spread**

**15g (½oz) caster sugar**

**70g (2½oz) hulled fresh strawberries, chopped (optional)**

**About 4 tablespoons skimmed milk, plus a little extra for glazing**

Britain can claim the scone as its own. Which part of the nation it originates from is unknown, but there are strong connections to Scotland, England and Ireland. This healthy version of the cream tea is just as tempting as the original.

1   Preheat the oven to 220°C/fan 200°C/gas mark 7. Lightly flour a non-stick baking sheet and set aside. Combine the flour, baking powder and cinnamon in a bowl. Rub in the sunflower spread until the mixture resembles breadcrumbs.

2   Stir in the sugar, strawberries (if using) and enough milk to form a soft dough. Lightly knead the dough on a lightly floured surface. Divide the dough into 4 equal portions and shape each one into a round that is about 6cm (2½in) in diameter. Place these on the prepared baking sheet and brush the tops with milk to glaze.

3   Bake for 10–12 minutes. Transfer to a wire rack to cool. Serve the scones warm or cold, split and spread with a little strawberry jam and top with fresh strawberry slices, if liked, or reduced-fat Greek-style yoghurt.

| per 100g | MED fat | LOW saturated fat | MED salt | MED sugar |
|---|---|---|---|---|
| per portion (% of GDA) | 159 kcal 8% | 4.7g fat 7% | 1.1g saturated fat 6% | 0.4g salt 7% | 6.1g sugars 7% |

# Strawberry sandwich cake

**Serves: 8**
**Preparation time: 20 minutes**
**Cooking time: 15–20 minutes**

**3 large eggs**

**75g (2¾oz) caster sugar**

**75g (2¾oz) plain flour, sifted, mixed with ½ teaspoon baking powder, sifted**

**For the filling:**

**3 tablespoons strawberry jam**

**150g (5½oz) sliced fresh strawberries**

This light, non-creamy version of the Victoria sponge is perfect for those special occasions, such as a birthday, for which only a good old-fashioned cake will do.

1 Preheat the oven to 180°C/fan 160°C/gas mark 4. Prepare 2 x 18cm (7in) sandwich tins. Grease with a little oil, then line the base with non-stick baking paper. Turn the paper over so that both sides are oiled.

2 Separate the eggs into two large grease-free bowls. Add the sugar to the yolks and whisk with a hand-held electric whisk until the mix is very pale and fluffy. This will take about 5 minutes – don't be impatient, as the more volume of air you add at this point, the lighter your cake will be.

3 Thoroughly wash and dry the whisks to remove all signs of grease, then whisk the egg whites until stiff peaks form. Mix a little of the whites into the yolks-and-sugar mixture to loosen the mix. Then use a large metal spoon to alternately fold the flour and egg whites into the yolks-and-sugar mixture, working very gently until it is all combined, with no flour left visible.

4 Spoon an equal quantity of the mixture into each prepared tin and bake for 15–20 minutes until slightly risen, golden and springy to the touch. The edges will also have shrunk from the sides slightly.

5 Allow to cool slightly, then remove the cakes from the tins and cool completely on a wire rack. Spread the jam over one cake, then add the sliced strawberries in an even layer. Now sandwich the cakes together.

**Cook's tip:** Remember – the more you whisk, the better the end result. Use a hand-held electric whisk if you can. And be as gentle as possible when folding through the flour to retain as much air in the cake as you can.

**Variation:** Dust the top with 2 tablespoons sifted icing sugar, if desired.

| per 100g | MED fat | LOW saturated fat | LOW salt | HIGH sugar |
|---|---|---|---|---|
| per portion (% of GDA) | **150 kcal** 8% | **3.5g fat** 5% | **1g saturated fat** 5% | **0.2g salt** 3% | **18.2g sugars** 20% |

# Index

# Acknowledgements

**The British Heart Foundation** would like to thank Anne Sheasby, Rae Ward, Moyra Fraser, Lizzie Harris and Deborah Kespert for their recipes.

**Simon & Schuster Illustrated** would like to thank the British Heart Foundation for their help and support.

**Picture credit:**